VOLTAIRE: CANDIDE

by

W. H. BARBER

Professor of French
Birkbeck College, University of London

EDWARD ARNOLD

© W. H. Barber 1960

First published 1960
by Edward Arnold (Publishers) Ltd.,
25 Hill Street, London W1X 8LL

Reprinted 1963, 1965, 1968, 1972, 1974, 1977

ISBN: 0 7131 5511 6

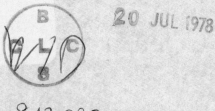

Printed in Great Britain by
The Camelot Press Ltd, Southampton

Contents

"I had rather have a fool to make me merry than experience to make me sad: and to travel for it too!"

Shakespeare, *As You Like It*, Act IV, Scene 1.

NOTE

The text of *Candide* quoted is that of the last edition to be revised by Voltaire. This was published in 1771, and is reproduced in the critical edition by René Pomeau, Paris, Nizet, 1959.

For Voltaire's letters, references are given, in the form 'Best. D' followed by the serial number of the letter, to *The Complete Works of Voltaire*, vol. 85: *Correspondence and related documents*, definitive edition by Theodore Besterman (Geneva and Thorpe Mandeville, 1968).

The spelling has been modernized in all quotations from the French.

Foreground

Odd as it would seem in the publicity-conscious world of to-day, two hundred years ago it was possible for an author of established European fame to launch a major work upon its career in almost total secrecy and under cover of an obscure pseudonym. 'Candide ou l'Optimisme, Traduit de l'allemand de Mr. le docteur Ralph' quietly made its appearance from anonymous printers in Geneva and Paris in the latter half of January 1759. Outside Voltaire's own household only two people, it seems, were admitted to the secret. In July 1758 Voltaire visited the Elector Palatine, Karl Theodor, at Schwetzingen, and entertained him, according to a likely tradition, with readings from Candide, on which he was then at work—just as, eleven years earlier, he had amused the Duchesse du Maine and her friends at Sceaux by reading from Zadig and perhaps other tales. And, in the autumn of that year, Voltaire apparently sent a manuscript version of his tale (which has only recently been rediscovered in the Bibliothèque de l'Arsenal in Paris) to one of his Parisian friends, the Duc de la Vallière.

From all others, Candide's existence remained concealed: the first mention it received in Voltaire's vast correspondence is in a note to Jacob Vernes in February 1759 (Best. D8119), complaining that 'je ne sais quel Candide, qui est une plaisanterie d'écolier' is being attributed to him; and later references in the early months of that year either disclaim any knowledge of the book, or find other authors for it. Indeed, Voltaire shortly afterwards sent his Genevan printer, Gabriel Cramer, three notes (Best. D8141, 8148, 8152), potentially for the public eye, implying total ignorance of 'une brochure intitulée Candide qu'on débite dit-on avec scandale, et qu'on dit venir de Lyon' (Best. D8141)

Such comically machiavellian precautions were not unnecessary, for the official reaction to Candide was immediately hostile; by the end of

February the authorities in both Geneva and Paris had taken action to suppress it, as 'rempli de principes dangereux par rapport à la Religion, et tendant à la dépravation des mœurs' (Best. Appendix D173. ii: Genevan Council minute). Measures of this sort were notoriously ineffective, especially in France, in preventing the circulation of heterodox works, but far less so, as Voltaire knew by harsh experience, in bringing misfortune upon an identifiable author or publisher.

Having thus established his defences, Voltaire was in a position to watch with satisfaction the mounting success of his book. Helped, no doubt, by the free publicity which official proscription always brings, and even more so by the rapid spread of the truth about its authorship *Candide* quickly became the best-seller of the century. Some twenty different editions (mostly, of course, piratical), together with an English and an Italian translation, were published in 1759 alone, and at least 50 had appeared before Voltaire's death in 1778. Whatever its origins, such success clearly went far beyond the limits of a mere *succès de scandale*; and our chief purpose in this essay must be to try to uncover the intrinsic qualities which ultimately account for it. *Candide*, however, is not merely an eighteenth-century best-seller: it has continued to be widely read to this day, becoming for posterity, when Voltaire's tragedy and epic have disappeared from all but the scholar's view, its author's characteristic work of art. This judgment of history upon a masterpiece of irony is in itself ironical, for Voltaire's own claim to immortality was made as the author of *La Henriade* and the true heir of Corneille and Racine. It is a judgment, however, which the most sympathetic study of Voltaire's work in the 'noble' genres can only confirm. Not only is *Candide* a more satisfying and vital work of art than any Voltairian tragedy; it achieves that vitality because, as we shall see, it has its roots at a far deeper level in the author's personality. The emotions, the intellectual conflicts which the book unfolds, are profoundly Voltaire's own, and its writing represents perhaps the most successful synthesis of three essential aspects of his nature: his compassion for humanity, his critical intellect, and his literary vocation.

This strongly personal aspect may seem strange at first glance in a work whose authorship Voltaire was reluctant to admit (although it was attributed to 'M. de Volt★★★', in an unauthorized edition, as early as 1759, it was first openly acknowledged by Voltaire himself only in a collected edition of his works which began publication, with his collaboration, in Geneva in 1768). The practical reasons of prudence behind this reluctance were certainly strong; but Voltaire was also, undoubtedly, reluctant to associate himself too openly with a work which belonged to a literary genre then still scarcely worthy of serious consideration. In spite of the changes in outlook which were growing and spreading in every direction with gathering momentum, the eighteenth century was still influenced by the literary traditions of French classicism, among which was the belief that prose fiction, if not actually harmful or contemptible (as some believed), had at any rate no claim to be taken seriously as art. The seventeenth-century theorists had omitted to legislate for it as they did for poetry and drama, and for the aspirant to literary immortality it had little indeed to offer in comparison with tragedy or epic.

For a man of Voltaire's standing and ambition in the nobler genres, such a work, all questions of orthodoxy apart, had necessarily to be played down as a mere *jeu d'esprit*, an amusing trifle of no consequence, if not disclaimed entirely. But these handicaps also conferred compensating advantages upon the novel. Having escaped the attention of the theorists, it possessed a freedom from convention and a flexibility which eighteenth-century drama, for instance, was struggling rather ineffectually to regain. Prose fiction thus offered the writer two major facilities not available in the grander forms; its humble status and accepted triviality made it an excellent vehicle for the launching of the intellectual squib, the unorthodox criticism, by the author who had, or aspired to, some public or literary standing (thus Montesquieu published the *Lettres Persanes* anonymously and later talked of the book as a youthful folly); and its freedom from established convention allowed it to be treated experimentally and individually, to become the means of a more direct and intimate expression of the author's own personality and its problems (the outstanding example here is Diderot). Voltaire takes full advantage of such possibilities in *Candide*.

The triviality, in the accepted view, of the prose tale has a bearing also upon another question concerning *Candide*. The conception of the work as a mere *jeu d'esprit* has encouraged legends about its genesis which are certainly misleading. According to one contemporary, *Candide* was begun during the few weeks of Voltaire's visit to Schwetzingen, and each chapter read to the Elector as it was finished. Another tradition, of unknown authenticity, pictures Voltaire, a few months later, shutting himself in his study and completing the tale in three days of uninterrupted, hectic writing. The truth here is not easy to find: Voltaire was ready to confide in his friends over his problems, even to discuss individual lines of verse, when he was writing a tragedy; but *Candide* he never mentioned to them. It is possible, however, sometimes to catch an indirect glimpse of Voltaire at work, through the reflection of one of his literary activities in the pages of another—in the use, perhaps, in an imaginative work of incidents or settings derived from historical researches which he was pursuing at the same period, or the occurrence in his letters of phrases or allusions also employed in the book on which he was engaged. Such evidence is inevitably flimsy, but in the absence of anything more solid it at least offers a pointer to where the truth may lie. The latest scholarly editor of *Candide*, M. René Pomeau, has found a number of indications of this sort which suggest that Voltaire may have begun his tale in January 1758. To quote only two examples: the cannibals and Jesuits of Paraguay, the Dutch colony of Surinam, which have their part to play in *Candide*, figure also in a chapter of Voltaire's major historical work, the *Essai sur les Mœurs*, which we know from his correspondence that he was writing in that month; and the celebrated phrase, in chapter 23 of *Candide*, describing France and England as at war 'pour quelques arpents de neige vers le Canada', is a slightly modified version of a remark in a letter dated 12 February 1758 (Best. D7630).

If we thus accept the possibility that *Candide* was begun in January

1758, a year before its publication, no less than four stages in its composition may be postulated, with varying degrees of assurance: January, at Lausanne; July, at Schwetzingen; a date in the autumn (as certain details suggest) when the complete manuscript version sent to the Duc de la Vallière was prepared; and a final revision, probably in early December just before the book went to press, which may have been the occasion of the non-stop three-day session. What has often been taken, then, to be a literary trifle, dashed off at first to amuse a princely patron and finished later in a sudden burst of energy, proves likely, in fact, to be a maturely considered work of art, developed and revised from time to time over the course of a whole year. Nor, indeed, was this the end of the process, for Voltaire made some additions to his tale (notably in chapter 22) in 1761, and introduced a few minor corrections in two subsequent editions.

In spite, then, of camouflage, *Candide* appears to be a piece of writing which Voltaire himself took seriously. It will emerge, I hope, in the course of this study how intimately concerned its author was with the themes and issues which it discusses—one is tempted, indeed, to wonder whether the fact that they touched him so closely may not have been one of the reasons behind Voltaire's reluctance to be publicly associated with it; the French classical tradition, to which he belonged, regarded the poet or the dramatist as a public figure, and did not look for an exposition of private thoughts and feelings in his works. But before we discuss its significance for Voltaire, and its relevance to his age, important and illuminating as these questions are for an understanding of the book, we must first ask what kind of a book it is, what it has to say, and what means the author uses to achieve his purposes.

If *Candide*, when it first appeared, had come into the hands of the unreflecting reader who consumes novels in rapid succession just for the entertainment of following a tale (and such readers existed in the eighteenth century as to-day), he or she might, just imaginably, have been naïve enough to suppose that this was merely another adventure story of a quite familiar variety. For more than a century, the vast majority of novels had been narratives, like *Candide*, of an episodic kind, describing the multifarious adventures of a central character or a small group of characters, loosely strung together, with numerous digressions, full of rapid movement, but lacking a plot of the dramatic sort such as the nineteenth-century novel made popular, and with little psychological interest. A hundred years earlier, such works had largely catered for the current taste for epic grandeur, dealing with the noble exploits in love and war of princes and antique heroes; but a humbler form had also grown up, known from its Spanish origins as the picaresque novel, which described the adventures, sometimes ludicrous, of a character of more lowly status, often a country lad making his way in the world by his wits—comedy to the heroic novel's tragedy, according to classical conceptions. The French masterpiece in this genre, Lesage's *Gil Blas*, was in fact completed in 1735, less than twenty-five years before the appearance of *Candide*. A further type of episodic novel, nearer to everyday reality than the heroic, more serious than the picaresque, would also be familiar to the reader whom we have in mind. Owing something to other fictional forms but something also to the fashion at the end of the seventeenth century for historical memoirs (authentic, embroidered, or purely imaginary), this depicted the adventures, often tragic, of a sympathetic central figure, against a background of contemporary or nearly contemporary life, sometimes made more vivid by the introduction of authentically historical scenes. The best known example here is afforded by the Abbé Prévost's highly successfully *Cleveland* (1731–9, 8 vols.), which has as its hero an imaginary illegitimate son of Oliver Cromwell—a melancholy figure, persecuted by his father and driven across half the world by a cruel pursuing fate.

With such fictional traditions, and especially perhaps with the picaresque novel, *Candide* has a good deal in common, at any rate superficially. Its hero, a naïve lad whose origins are relatively obscure in more senses than one, is launched into a series of adventures and misfortunes, haphazardly linked together, which take him from Westphalia to Constantinople by way of Portugal and Paraguay. Around him are collected a number of episodic characters and a smaller group, mostly from his Westphalian home, whom he is frequently parted from and then encounters again, usually by chance; chief among whom is his beloved Cunégonde. There are digressions of the traditional sort, informing us of the previous adventures of new episodic characters (the longest here, 'l'histoire de la Vieille', fills chapters 11 and 12). Many of the most banal incidents of traditional fiction are duly introduced: characters are shipwrecked (chap. 5), captured by pirates (chaps. 12, 27) and by cannibals (chap. 16), sold into slavery (chaps. 12, 27), imprisoned and condemned by arbitrary rulers (chaps. 6, 28), robbed in inns and swindled by chance acquaintances (chaps. 10, 22); they encounter each other by the strangest of coincidences, and in the most unexpected disguises (chaps. 4, 7, 12, 24, 26, 27, 30). Moreover, in spite of the fanciful extremes of fortune to which the characters are subjected, their adventures are linked from time to time to historical events: the Lisbon earthquake of 1755, the execution of Admiral Byng, Damiens's attempted assassination of Louis XV.

Candide, however, is anything but a naïve tale, and one does not have to look very far to see that in it Voltaire is using the familiar traditions of prose fiction in pursuit of his own particular ends, and giving them some rather odd twists in the process.

For one thing, it has nothing of the leisureliness of the old episodic novel. Cleveland's travels fill eight volumes, and *Gil Blas* originally appeared in four, but *Candide*, in its first edition a single duodecimo of under 300 pages, is a short novel even by modern standards. The general effect is, deliberately, one of compression: the hero is hurried on at breakneck speed from one country to the next, from one misfortune, often, to another, and the background to his adventures is sketched only in the briefest terms. It is as though Voltaire is caricaturing the adventure novel by this means, just as in the early cinema the chase scenes were made more comic by artificially speeding up the film.

This suggests a deliberate attempt to undermine the illusion of reality which the straightforward adventure story strives to create for the reader;

and the impression is strengthened when we look at further aspects of the tale.

To take one instance, the introduction of historical events was traditionally employed, obviously, to enhance the illusion of reality; and here, when the public events introduced had all occurred less than four years before the novel appeared, one might perhaps have looked for a topical authenticity which the reader himself could check from his own experience. In fact, however, the facts are mixed with fantasy: no Bulgarian troops (nor any others) were fighting in Westphalia in the months before the Lisbon earthquake, and of the six ex-monarchs whom Candide encounters at Venice in what must apparently be 1757, two were by then dead. Similarly, Candide in his South American wanderings, as he flees from the agents of the Inquisition in Buenos Aires and then from the Jesuits of Paraguay, penetrates into an unknown and ideal land. Such a visit had figured often enough in fiction: Cleveland discovers a Utopian community in the remoteness of St. Helena: the difference here is that after the topical realities which form the background of his movements up to this point, Candide now reaches a realm which is clearly intended to be nothing but a vision. Voltaire calls it Eldorado, and by later allusions makes it clear that it has no place in the real world (e.g. Martin says, chap. 20: 'je vous avoue qu'en jetant la vue sur ce globe, ou plutôt ce globule, je pense que Dieu l'a abandonné à quelque être malfaisant; j'en excepte toujours Eldorado'.)

It would be difficult, again, to accept the events of the narrative as plausible fiction, let alone reality: the misfortunes of Candide and his companions are for the most part credible enough, taken singly; but they are piled up in such bizarre abundance, and so rapidly, that even the most naïve reader must become incredulous, and Voltaire's intention of parodying the picaresque novel becomes clear. To take one highly compressed example: chapters 11 and 12 form a digression of the familiar type —'La Vieille' tells her life history during the voyage to Buenos Aires. The narrative of an Italian princess captured by corsairs and sold into slavery in North Africa is acceptable enough, within the fictional convention. But Voltaire first cheats his readers of the conventional escape from this predicament—the princess is rescued from a scene of carnage in Morocco by a eunuch from Naples who proves, by the inevitable coincidence, to be a former devoted servant of her family; but, promising to send her back to Italy, he promptly sells her as a slave in Algiers. And then, leaving conventional plausibility behind, the author whirls the princess eastwards, from one slave-owner to another, until she finds herself with the janissaries besieged by Russian troops at Azov, appeases the cannibalism of the starving garrison by the grimly ludicrous sacrifice of a buttock, and ultimately makes her way westwards again via Moscow and a wretched progress through the inn-kitchens of north-east Europe. This is epic adventure held down to the level of the sordid; and Voltaire ends his digression with an open reminder of its banal artificiality—'Je ne vous aurais même jamais parlé de mes malheurs . . . s'il n'était d'usage dans un vaisseau de conter des histoires pour se désennuyer'.

Other aspects of the narrative point to the same conclusion. Major fictional events in the tale are lightheartedly repudiated when necessary: the reader is given no reason to suspect, at the time, that Pangloss has not been efficiently hanged by the Inquisition in chapter 6, nor that the Baron is not dead after Candide's swordthrust in chapter 15: but both are nevertheless resurrected, and provided with mockingly implausible explanations of their survival, because Voltaire has need of their presence at the end of his tale.

Another element of parody is visible, too, in the exaggerated violence of emotion which the characters display in the conventional situations of fiction. The clandestine meeting of Candide and Cunégonde in Don Issacar's house in Lisbon is the stock recognition scene with effects heightened till they topple over:

> La vieille reparut bientôt; elle soutenait avec peine une femme tremblante, d'une taille majestueuse, brillante de pierreries, et couverte d'un voile. 'Ôtez ce voile' dit la vieille à Candide. Le jeune homme approche; il lève le voile d'une main timide. Quel moment! quelle surprise! il croit voir mademoiselle Cunégonde, il la voyait en effet, c'était elle-même. La force lui manque, il ne peut proférer une parole,

B

il tombe à ses pieds. Cunégonde tombe sur le canapé. La vieille les
accable d'eaux spiritueuses; ils reprennent leurs sens, ils se parlent:
ce sont d'abord des mots entrecoupés, des demandes et des réponses
qui se croisent, des soupirs, des larmes, des cris.

And then the bubble of emotion is neatly pricked by a matter-of-fact
recall to common prudence—'La vieille leur recommande de faire moins
de bruit, et les laisse en liberté' (chap. 7). Again, later on in the tale,
Candide has apparently lost Cunégonde for ever and, having just killed
her brother the Jesuit baron, is in flight with Cacambo across unknown
country, when he refuses all food in an outburst of suicidal grief worthy
of one of the Abbé Prévost's heroes: 'à quoi me servira de prolonger mes
misérables jours, puisque je dois les traîner loin d'elle dans les remords et
dans le désespoir?' (chap. 16). The impact upon the reader of this tragic
utterance in the grand manner is carefully modified, however, by the
fact that in the previous sentence Voltaire has made Candide explain
matters in plain factual language: 'Comment veux-tu, disait Candide,
que je mange du jambon, quand j'ai tué le fils de monsieur le baron, et
que je me vois condamné à ne revoir la belle Cunégonde de ma vie?' The
bathos of this contrast, moreover, would be even more striking for an
eighteenth-century Frenchman than it is for the modern reader, for the
classical tradition in French taste insisted that anything so material and
homely as 'du jambon' was jarringly out of place in a description of
noble and tragic emotion.

A similar unwillingness to create living illusion is visible in Voltaire's
treatment of the characters themselves. The episodic novel had never, of
course, progressed beyond what in modern eyes is a rudimentary stage in
characterization; simple stereotypes for the most part sufficed so long as
the central interest was in events rather than in psychological analysis.
But even by such standards the characterization here is decidedly per-
functory; Candide and Cunégonde, in their simplicity, are the mere
outlines of a conventional hero and heroine, and most of the other
characters can be adequately described in a phrase: the Baron is a choleric
snob, Martin a stoical pessimist, Cacambo a faithful servant, the Old

Woman another Cunégonde in disillusioned old age (the only exception here is perhaps Pangloss, for reasons which will become apparent later). And this impression is supported by the kind of names Voltaire gives his characters. The only character in the novel to possess a realistically complete set of names is the haughty Spanish nobleman who is governor of Buenos Aires: Don Fernando d'Ibaraa, y Figueora, y Mascarenes, y Lampourdos, y Souza; and his name, as Voltaire points out, is all the description that he needs. For the rest, single names suffice: these are sometimes descriptive surnames, as in an allegory—Candide, Pangloss ('all tongue'), Pococurante ('caring little'), sometimes plain first names— Jacques, Martin, Paquette, Cunégonde; often the characters are known not by name at all, but by descriptive epithets—le Baron, la Vieille, le Grand Inquisiteur, l'abbé périgourdin. It is clear that we are not being encouraged to regard these characters as human beings conceived after the complex pattern of reality; they are no more than puppets, some of them puppets capable of making only one particular gesture, and the author does not wish us to take them for anything else.

This niggardliness in the gift of life to his characters plainly helps Voltaire in his purpose of parodying the episodic adventure novel; it makes it easier for the reader to withdraw from that sympathetic participation which is essential for the effectiveness of ordinary narrative fiction; it makes it possible for him, consequently, to view characters and narrative as it were externally, and consequently *critically*—to become aware of the caricature and exaggeration, the deliberate implausibilities, the bathetic contrasts, which Voltaire employs in making fun of a naïve and hackneyed genre. But there is much more in *Candide* than parody. If the characters in the tale are puppets, to what purpose are they being manipulated? If the reader is not to take too seriously the adventures of the people in the story, where does the book's real centre of interest lie?

The answer, of course, is to be found in the tale's alternative title— l'*Optimisme*. The episodic adventure story is merely the outward shape in which Voltaire has chosen to present what is essentially a personal comment on a religious and philosophical problem of great concern both to himself and to his contemporaries. These wider aspects of the subject we shall return to later; for the moment, we must first consider what the problem was and how it informs the structure of *Candide*.

To Voltaire and the many contemporaries who shared his belief in a rational deity, 'l'Être Suprême', who had created in his own image a universe ordered by rational and universal laws, the existence of evil and suffering in the world presented a serious theological difficulty. Incontrovertible blemishes in creation argued some deficiency either in divine benevolence, or in divine omnipotence, and such deficiencies seemed rationally incompatible with the necessary notion of God's perfection. Of the many attempts at a way out of this dilemma which have been made (and the problem, in one form or another, is clearly as old as theism itself), Voltaire is here concerned with three: first, the view that evil has no absolute existence, but is merely a means to good and consequently part of God's benevolent scheme of things (this is 'Optimism'); secondly, the belief that evil is real and inherent in the world, because in a universe torn between supernatural forces of good and evil, God has given it over to an evil power; and thirdly, the attitude that the problem is intellectually insoluble, that speculation on the subject is vain, and man is better otherwise employed.

Round these three points of view the intellectual structure of the book is formed. The first, that of 'Optimism', is the doctrine professed by Dr. Pangloss, and in which Candide and Cunégonde are brought up. The second is that of the 'Manichean' Martin; while the third is the conclusion to which Candide is finally brought at the end of the tale. The argument thus has a clear dialectic pattern: the conflict between two opposing speculative theories is resolved by a conclusion which transcends them both by its new awareness of their common inadequacy.

It would be dangerously paradoxical, however, as well as misleading, to pursue in such abstract terms discussion of a book which is primarily intended to poke fun at abstract speculation. What is important, once the intellectual issues are clear, is to see how the author has shaped his narrative to fit them. One may indeed ask 'why employ a narrative at all? is not this material for a philosophical essay rather than for fiction?' But the answer, and with it perhaps the reason for Voltaire's outstanding success, lies precisely in the nature of the debate itself. What Candide receives in childhood from Pangloss is a mere *theory*, an interpretation of existence whose validity rests solely on the fact that it is held to offer an .ntellectually satisfying answer to an abstract speculative problem; what Candide has achieved at the end of his adventures is a practical basis for living which has nothing to do with speculation but is exclusively the product of his own *experience*. The function of the fictional narrative is thus clear; it shows us Candide testing Pangloss's theories against reality; and it provides him with the personal knowledge of life which constitutes the foundation for his conclusion. The story is thus of the essence of the debate: it offers us a yardstick with which to assess abstract theories, and it ultimately furnishes us with a constructive means of escape from the dilemma.

It is necessary, then, to look rather more closely at the events of the narrative and the nature of their impact on Candide himself—for he remains at the centre throughout: conflicting theories contend for his adherence, and he is the author's spokesman at the end of the tale.

The first stage of his career is spent in the happy seclusion of the Château de Thunder-ten-tronckh—for its inhabitants (who know nothing better, if also nothing worse) it is a second Eden, in which it is easy to believe Pangloss's pronouncements that 'tout est au mieux . . . dans ce meilleur des mondes possibles', and Candide for one accepts them 'avec toute la bonne foi de son âge et de son caractère'.

In the many misfortunes that follow rapidly upon his expulsion from this 'paradis terrestre' for having presumed to kiss Cunégonde, Candide continues to believe that all is for the best: his faith in the beneficence of Providence and in the goodness of human nature survives his horrific experiences as a Bulgarian soldier, and when he encounters kindness in Holland from the Anabaptist Jacques, he readily seizes upon it as evidence of the truth of Pangloss's teaching (chap. 3).

A less optimistic view is first expressed in the tale when Candide,

Pangloss and Jacques are sailing to Lisbon: Jacques insists, arguing with Pangloss, that 'il faut bien que les hommes aient un peu corrompu la nature, car ils ne sont pas nés loups, et ils sont devenus loups' (chap. 4); but it takes the combined horrors of the Lisbon earthquake and the ensuing auto-da-fé to make Candide doubt the truth of Pangloss's philosophy, and question the beneficial purpose of the evil he has experienced—'Si c'est ici le meilleur des mondes possibles, que sont donc les autres?' (chap. 6).

Subsequently, his attitude varies a good deal with circumstances. When his own prospects for once appear bright, his youthful resilience reasserts itself, and he is ready again to agree with Pangloss, in some degree at any rate; when he and Cunégonde are on the voyage to Buenos Aires, reunited and with their Portuguese misfortunes behind them, he hopefully proclaims, to a less confident Cunégonde, 'c'est certainement le nouveau monde qui est le meilleur des univers possibles' (chap. 10); and the final news that Cunégonde awaits him in Constantinople calls forth a triumphant cry—'Mon cher Martin, encore une fois, Pangloss avait raison. Tout est bien.' But his despair can be equally extreme: the sufferings of the negro slave in Surinam move him profoundly—'O Pangloss! s'écria Candide, tu n'avais pas diviné cette abomination: c'en est fait, il faudra qu'à la fin je renonce à ton optimisme' (chap. 19); and disappointment at failing to find Cunégonde and Cacambo waiting for him when he arrives in Venice casts him into 'une mélancolie noire' in which he feels that 'tout n'est qu'illusion et calamité', that 'il valait mieux rester dans le paradis du Dorado que de revenir dans cette maudite Europe'.

All the time however, in spite of a tendency to favour the optimistic view which is the result partly of Pangloss's teaching, and partly, it seems, of a naturally cheerful temperament, Candide is subjected to the inexorable pressure of experience. The process is one of continual disillusionment; the extent of the evil and suffering in the world is something which he naturally minimizes until personal knowledge teaches him better; the innocent Candide is continually proved wrong. Not only does he find it ever more difficult to fit the misfortunes he himself experiences and observes into the optimistic scheme, to believe that they have an ultimately beneficent purpose: it is also brought home to him time and again that the sum total of human misery is vastly greater than he could have imagined, that men are much unhappier even than they seem.

Of these two aspects of Candide's disillusionment, the first is of course exemplified by some of the most celebrated episodes in the book: the optimists' attempts to see a beneficent purpose behind the indiscriminate slaughter of the Lisbon earthquake or of the Seven Years' War (thinly disguised by Voltaire as that between the 'Bulgares' and 'Abares') are clearly an affront to human suffering; and human bigotry, religious and judicial, can act with equal cruelty, as the Portuguese auto-da-fé and the execution of Admiral Byng illustrate. Two comparatively minor incidents, however, are perhaps really even more telling. The virtuous Anabaptist, Jacques, is drowned off Lisbon as a result of his successful rescue of a brutal and vicious sailor, who had previously attacked him, who makes no attempt to save him, and who is the only survivor, with Candide and Pangloss, when the ship sinks a few moments later (chap. 5). In spite of Pangloss, who 'proves' that 'la rade de Lisbonne avait été formée exprès pour que cet anabaptiste s'y noyât', such active malevolence of fate leaves Candide bewildered. Later on, the harsh and unscrupulous Vanderdendur, who had stolen the bulk of Candide's treasure from Eldorado, drowns when his ship is sunk by a vessel which he had attacked; Candide feels for a moment that Providence is justified, but he has no answer to Martin's objection: 'Vous voyez, dit Candide à Martin, que le crime est puni quelquefois: ce coquin de patron hollandais a eu le sort qu'il méritait.—Oui, dit Martin; mais fallait-il que les passagers qui étaient sur le vaisseau périssent aussi?' (chap. 20). Events seem to lack any discernible moral purpose or rational pattern, not merely where the broad forces of nature or of history are predominant, but also at the level of the individual and his immediate circle.

The second aspect of Candide's disillusionment is one which, if less obviously striking, is none the less strongly emphasized by frequent reiteration. Inclined as he is to the optimistic view, Candide tends to assume that all is well unless he is given plain evidence to the contrary, to believe that people are content, and have led happy lives, if they show no obvious signs of distress. This attitude is soon undermined by what he learns of the experience of others; and here the conventional device of the digression is used by Voltaire very appositely to serve the purpose of his argument: whenever a character relates his or her experiences, they always reveal unforeseen depths of misfortune. Often, indeed, they are introduced by means of a kind of wager. We hear that Cunégonde cannot believe that anyone could have endured more suffering than she has herself (chap. 10)—and she is shown to be wrong. All the other passengers in the ship to Buenos Aires, too (though we are happily spared the details), have tales to tell which force Cunégonde and Candide to admit the truth of La Vieille's forecast, that there would not be one of them 'qui n'ait souvent maudit sa vie, qui ne se soit souvent dit à lui-même qu'il était le plus malheureux des hommes' (chap. 12). Later on, Candide chooses Martin as his travelling companion by advertising in Surinam for 'un honnête homme qui voudrait faire le voyage avec lui, à condition que cet homme serait le plus dégoûté de son état et le plus malheureux de la province'—and in listening to the stories of the twenty most eligible candidates whom he selects from among the vast crowd which presents itself, he remembers La Vieille and her prophecy on the voyage—and also thinks of Pangloss: 'Ce Pangloss, disait-il, serait bien embarrassé à démontrer son système. Je voudrais qu'il fût ici. Certainement si tout va bien, c'est dans Eldorado, et non pas dans le reste de la terre' (chap. 19). Crowned heads themselves are not exempt from misery (chap. 26), and even the apparently fortunate have their private wretchedness: in chapter 24, Candide loses his bet with Martin that the young couple whom they notice arm in arm in St. Mark's Square in Venice are as happy as they look. Paquette and Frère Giroflée each have as sad a tale to tell as any others Candide has heard.

The process of disillusion is thus central to the main argument of the book; but it is also introduced, as though to form a parallel accompaniment strengthening the theme, in a number of contexts not immediately concerned with the discussion of optimism and the problem of evil. Candide begins by regarding the Château de Thunder-ten-tronckh as 'le plus beau des châteaux possibles', as 'le paradis terrestre'—until he visits Eldorado; his naïve acceptance of the Bulgarian recruiting officer's flattering hospitality lands him immediately in irons; he is almost equally rudely disappointed in his confident expectations of ready help from the wealthy and pious inhabitants of Holland; later in the tale he is all too easily impressed by the extreme fastidiousness of taste of the blasé Pococurante, until Martin reminds him that 'les meilleurs estomacs ne sont pas ceux qui rebutent tous les aliments' (chap. 25). Worst of all, the romantic quest for 'la belle Cunégonde', which directly or indirectly motivates almost all Candide's travels, is doomed to end in disillusion: when he is finally reunited with her at Constantinople she is 'horriblement laide'. Nothing of Candide's youthful vision of a world of happiness is allowed to remain.

Candide's naïve faith in the facile optimism of Pangloss is thus overwhelmed by the mounting weight of his own experience of a very different reality; to this extent, he moves much nearer to accepting the universal pessimism of Martin, the belief that the world is the devil's work, created only 'pour nous faire enrager'. And yet he never finally does so. The reason perhaps is the same as that which makes him incapable of shutting his eyes to the facts and accepting Pangloss's comforting illusions: both optimism and Martin's Manichean pessimism are ultimately passive attitudes—they involve merely accepting things as they are, justifying the existing situation by means of speculative theories which, comforting or depressing according to taste, unite in tempting the individual to sink into indifference and lethargy by denying all prospect of any improvement whatever. A world which, for all its evil, is *already* 'le meilleur des mondes possibles' is as much a world of blank despair as one malevolently created 'pour nous faire enrager'. But Candide himself continues, in spite of every setback, to cling to an active philosophy of hope, to struggle on towards better things even in the worst of misfortunes—a hope symbolized throughout, of course, by his quest for Cunégonde, and one which he refuses to abandon even when the quest itself has ended in disillusion. Inevitably, therefore, he remains dissatisfied with the views of both Pangloss and Martin; but not until the last pages of the tale does he find the solution which allows him to put them both behind him.

Constantinople brings the end of the travellers' major misfortunes; but it merely replaces them by an idle existence, enlivened only by philosophical disputation, and boredom (which had destroyed all pleasure for Pococurante) soon makes them all wonder whether their earlier sufferings were not to be preferred. Two further incidents are needed before a true dénouement can be reached, for two questions still remain unanswered. The first of these is the philosophical one: how are we to understand the world? where can we find a rationally satisfactory answer to the problem of existence and the problem of evil? The answers come, in no uncertain terms, from 'un derviche très fameux, qui passait pour le meilleur philosophe de la Turquie', whom Pangloss, Martin and Candide consult.

> Pangloss porta la parole, et lui dit 'Maître, nous venons vous prier de nous dire pourquoi un aussi étrange animal que l'homme a été formé?'—'De quoi te mêles-tu?' dit le derviche, 'est-ce là ton affaire?'—'Mais, mon révérend père,' dit Candide, 'il y a horriblement de mal sur la terre'.—'Qu'importe,' dit le derviche, 'qu'il y ait du mal ou du bien? Quand sa hautesse envoie un vaisseau en Égypte, s'embarrasse-t-elle si les souris qui sont dans le vaisseau sont à leur aise ou non?'—'Que faut-il donc faire?' dit Pangloss.—'Te taire,' dit le derviche.—'Je me flattais', dit Pangloss, 'de raisonner un peu avec vous des effets et des causes, du meilleur des mondes possibles, de l'origine du mal, de la nature de l'âme, et de l'harmonie préétablie.' Le derviche à ces mots leur ferma la porte au nez [chap. 30].

If metaphysical speculation is idle folly, because there are no grounds for assuming that the universe has a rational purpose which takes account of man, one part of Candide's debate is clearly eliminated—the theories of Pangloss and Martin are equally worthless; but the practical problem of human happiness remains. How can man best order his daily existence? Here Voltaire has already prepared the ground by the picture he has given us, at the beginning of his chapter, of the boredom of the reunited characters now that their adventures are over; the point is finally made through Candide's encounter with another sage. The 'bon vieillard' whose modest prosperity, tranquil independence, and sturdy ignorance of public affairs make such a favourable impression on Candide has a simple lesson to impart: his secret is not wealth, but work. ' "Vous devez avoir," dit Candide au Turc, "une vaste et magnifique terre?"— "Je n'ai que vingt arpents," répondit le Turc; "je les cultive avec mes enfants; le travail éloigne de nous trois grands maux, l'ennui, le vice et le besoin".' And once Candide has by this means come to realize that 'il faut cultiver notre jardin', all begins to go well with the little community; unsuspected practical talents emerge, which compensate for other failings—'Cunégonde était à la vérité bien laide; mais elle devint une excellente pâtissière'—and even the two philosophers, in their different ways, are reconciled to the new existence: Martin gloomily declares 'travaillons sans raisonner . . . c'est le seul moyen de rendre la vie supportable': and Pangloss, elated because all has turned out for the best after all, is ready to demonstrate that work is part of the divine purpose for mankind—'quand l'homme fut mis dans le jardin d'Eden, il y fut mis, *ut operaretur eum*, pour qu'il travaillât; ce qui prouve que l'homme n'est pas né pour le repos'.

By what, then, might at first glance seem a paradox, Voltaire concludes his attack on 'optimism' on a clear note of hope. Pangloss's optimism, indeed, is rejected precisely because it is a philosophy which denies all possibility of improving the world—'Si c'est ici le meilleur des mondes possibles, que sont donc les autres?' (chap. 6). Whatever harsh lessons Candide may have learned from experience, however plain it has been made that the utopian virtues of Eldorado are beyond the reach of ordinary men, he none the less retains the conviction that, as in his quest for Cunégonde, there is always room for hope. The conclusion shows him realizing that, on however modest a scale, it is possible for human beings to improve their lot by their own efforts, to create a haven of relative tranquillity and prosperity in a world largely given over to evil; but only providing that their energies are not frustrated by metaphysical doctrines which invite submission and inertia.

The narrative of *Candide* is thus a vehicle carefully designed to convey a philosophical discussion of topical concern both to author and reader, as well as being an entertaining parody of a familiar sort of novel; but it is also more. It has embedded in it elements of satire (including satire of the optimists themselves) which reflect Voltaire's hostility to various features of the contemporary scene—themes which for the most part are developed often elsewhere in his works, but which are also highly relevant in a tale in which the hero's experience of the world's wickedness and folly is of central importance.

The subject for satire to which Voltaire returns most frequently throughout his long career is that of organized religion in general, and the Roman Catholic Church in particular—the bigotry and intolerance of religious sects, the abuses and injustices to which superstition and greed for material advantage can lead where religious organizations have wealth and power. Here the subject is treated by Voltaire in highly characteristic fashion, and he relates it closely to his narrative. In Holland, the starving Candide discovers that a man who has just preached a sermon on charity is none the less capable of treating him anything but charitably because he does not denounce the Pope as Antichrist (chap. 3). In Portugal the Inquisition and its auto-da-fé appears as an inevitable concomitant of the Lisbon earthquake, because 'il était décidé par l'université de Coïmbre, que le spectacle de quelques personnes brûlées à petit feu en grande cérémonie, est un secret infaillible pour empêcher la terre de trembler' (chap. 6). And to this picture of superstition and cruelty is added a further feature: the Grand Inquisitor himself is shown as a dissolute and unscrupulous character, capable of blackmailing Don Issacar into an arrangement to share Cunégonde's favours between them on a strict weekly basis (chap. 8).

Again, the Jesuits of Paraguay enter naturally enough into Candide's adventures in South America—it is by enlisting as a captain in the Spanish army to fight against them that he is able to escape, for the moment, from the pursuit of the Inquisition—but they are used by Voltaire as a satirical example of the evils of priestcraft. In Paraguay their love of wealth and power has held unfettered sway—'Los Padres y ont tout, et les peuples rien; c'est le chef-d'œuvre de la raison et de la justice' (chap. 14)—and Voltaire makes much, not only of the discrepancy between the luxurious living of the Jesuits and the poverty of the natives, but also of the paradoxical situations which they have created by acquiring secular authority. Every Jesuit in Paraguay combines the professions of priest and soldier, as Cunégonde's brother explains to Candide—'Je fus honoré en arrivant du sousdiaconat et d'une lieutenance. Je suis aujourd'hui colonel et prêtre. Nous recevons vigoureusement les troupes du roi d'Espagne; je vous réponds qu'elles seront excommuniquées et battues' (chap. 15). And while in America the Jesuits make war on Spain and Portugal, in Europe they continue to provide confessors to those countries' sovereigns.

Monasticism, too, comes in for criticism on lines familiar to readers not merely of Voltaire's other works but of those of the writers of the French Enlightenment in general. It was an institution which they widely condemned as unnatural and harmful for the individual, injurious to society through its imposition of celibacy upon a substantial fraction of the population, and a tyrannous abuse when used by families (as it frequently was) as a means of cheaply shedding their responsibilities towards younger, or refractory, sons and daughters. For the further disillusionment of Candide, Frère Giroflée is introduced, in chapter 24, as yet another exemplar of the unhappiness which can underlie a smiling and contented outward appearance. Candide soon learns that Frère Giroflée's life is one of bitter frustration: forced by his parents to take vows as a boy in order to improve the financial prospects of his elder brother, he has nothing but hatred for the monastic life. 'La jalousie, la discorde, la rage habitent dans le couvent (...) quand je rentre le soir dans le monastère, je suis prêt de me casser la tête contre les murs du dortoir; et tous mes confrères sont dans le même cas.' Whatever the tribulations of life 'in the world', it is clear that they cannot be escaped by retiring into monastic seclusion.

A second satirical theme with which Voltaire was continually concerned was that of the horrors and folly of war, and this receives considerable emphasis in *Candide*. As an unwilling recruit in the Bulgarian army (chap. 2) he suffers the full harshness of a military discipline obviously modelled on the Prussian. In the subsequent battle against the 'Abares', the scene at first presents a gay appearance, with bright uniforms, cheerful music and orderly formations, but the cruel realities of war soon transform it into one of hideous chaos, described by Voltaire with unsparing realism. Candide thus receives a further disillusioning lesson in the grim facts of life and death—a lesson which is later reinforced by the descriptions he receives, from Pangloss (chap. 4) and the Baron (chap. 15), of the sacking of the Château de Thunder-ten-tronckh in the course of the same campaign. War is not here presented, however, as merely a manifestation of the human capacity for cruelty and brutality, disconcerting as that is for the optimistic view. The hypocrisy and self-deception which surround it, the folly and stupidity which cause it, are also indicted. When Candide has been inveigled into accepting the Bulgarian King's shilling the recruiting officers treat him as a hero, but take no risks with him: ' "C'en est assez," lui dit-on, " vous voilà l'appui, le soutien, le défenseur, le héros des Bulgares; votre fortune est faite, et votre gloire est assurée." On lui met sur le champ les fers aux pieds, et on le mène au régiment' (chap. 2). After the battle in chapter 3, *both* sides celebrate their 'victory' with a *Te Deum*. And the so-called 'laws of war', Voltaire suggests, are merely convenient devices for salving the consciences of rulers by lending a colour of respectable 'legality' to what is in fact atrocious. The most horrifying description in the book is that, in chapter 3, of the inhabitants of a village 'que les Bulgares avaient brûlé selon les lois du droit public'. And wars of this sort are fought for reasons of a triviality which makes a mockery of the suffering they cause. Martin's comment on the fighting in North America between France

and Britain has become famous: 'vous savez que ces deux nations sont
en guerre pour quelques arpents de neige vers le Canada, et qu'elles
dépensent pour cette belle guerre beaucoup plus que tout le Canada ne
vaut' (chap. 23).

Thirdly, Voltaire includes, in chapter 22, an account of Candide's
visit to Paris which gives him the opportunity for a satirical description
of the life of the capital, its follies and its vices. This contains much that
is personal to Voltaire, such as the discussion of the Parisian theatre, with
its praise of his favourite actress Mademoiselle Clairon and ridicule of
his enemy the critic Fréron; but much too is in a well-established tradition of social satire which goes back beyond Montesquieu's *Lettres
Persanes* of 1721 to the *Caractères* of La Bruyère (1688).

While such general satirical topics as these can be integrated quite
successfully into a narrative whose whole purpose is concerned with
revealing the darkest aspects of life to the innocent hero, there are
other subjects for satire which are more immediately related to the
central theme of the book. As we shall see later, the philosophy of
optimism which Voltaire is attacking is one which he closely associated
with Germany and his own experiences there, and which the general
public also connected with that country, since two of its best known
exponents were the German philosophers Leibniz and Wolff. Voltaire
consequently gives his tale a German setting: the Westphalia in which
Candide is born is a province whose wretchedness had shocked him, and
one which in its poverty and ignorance not only makes an ironic setting
for the Eden of Candide's innocence, but also offers an opportunity of
satirizing the hollow pretentiousness of the German nobility:

> Monsieur le Baron était un des plus puissants seigneurs de la West-
> phalie, car son château avait une porte et des fenêtres. Sa grande salle
> même était ornée d'une tapisserie. Tous les chiens de ses basses-cours
> composaient une meute dans le besoin; ses palefreniers étaient ses
> piqueurs; le vicaire du village était son grand aumônier. Ils l'appelaient
> tous *Monseigneur*, et ils riaient quand il faisait des contes [chap. 1].

This fatuous pride is again exemplified in Cunégonde's brother, the

Jesuit 'colonel et prêtre'. His obstinate refusal, whatever the circumstances, to allow his sister to marry Candide because, lacking the necessary '72 quartiers', he is socially beneath her, is the occasion first of his 'death' by Candide's sword in Paraguay (chap. 15) and finally of his being disposed of by Candide at Constantinople by being sold back as a galley-slave to his former owner, 'le lévanti patron' (chap. 30).

Further, the chief vehicle for Voltaire's satire on optimism is Pangloss, a caricature of the contemporary German professor of philosophy, the disciple of Leibniz and Wolff. Pangloss continually uses jargon which parodies the Wolffians. His subject is 'La métaphysico-theologo-cosmolonigologie'; his talk is of 'la raison suffisante', 'les futurs contingents', 'l'harmonie préétablie', and of course 'le meilleur des mondes possibles'—all terms which have their precise technical sense in the Leibnizian system. Needless to say, however, he is in fact a wretched exponent of Leibnizianism. He is prepared to take the optimistic view of the purpose of evil to the absurd length of arguing that 'les malheurs particuliers font le bien général, de sorte que plus il y a de malheurs particuliers, et plus tout est bien' (chap. 4). His views on freewill and determinism, which attract the attention of the Portuguese Inquisition in chapter 5, are nonsensical as well as heretical, without being very specifically Leibnizian. And his celebrated examples of the workings of a purposeful reason in the ordering of the universe—'Remarquez bien que les nez ont été faits pour porter les lunettes, aussi avons-nous des lunettes. Les jambes sont visiblement instituées pour être chaussées, et nous avons des chausses' (chap. 1)—caricature a line of argument which was very commonly employed in the early eighteenth century as a demonstration of the existence of God (the so-called argument from final causes), but it is one which has no special association with Leibniz or Wolff.

Pangloss, however, typifies for Voltaire many of the characteristics he found most detestable in all metaphysical philosophers, and in the German Wolffians in particular. His smug and fatuous dogmatism is outwardly proof against all argument and all experience:

'Eh bien, mon cher Pangloss,' lui dit Candide, ' quand vous avez été pendu, disséqué, roué de coups, et que vous avez ramé aux galères, avez-vous toujours pensé que tout allait le mieux du monde?'—'Je suis toujours de mon premier sentiment,' répondit Pangloss; 'car enfin je suis philosophe, il ne me convient pas de me dédire, Leibniz ne pouvant pas avoir tort, et l'harmonie préétablie étant d'ailleurs la plus belle chose du monde, aussi bien que le plein et la matière subtile' [chap. 28].

His preoccupation with the academic makes him capable of overlooking the most urgent human practical needs, as when amidst the ruins of Lisbon he treats Candide to a doctrinaire discourse on the causes of earthquakes instead of attending to his injuries (chap. 5). He is pedantically obsessed with facts for their own sake and delights in imparting useless information (e.g. his encyclopedic list of assassinated monarchs, chap. 30). Voltaire, moreover, could never bring himself to believe that metaphysicians of this sort were sincere in their dogmatism, and he accordingly makes Pangloss confess in the end that his optimism was a pose, maintained from vanity: 'Pangloss avouait, qu'il avait toujours horriblement souffert; mais ayant soutenu une fois que tout allait à merveilles, il le soutenait toujours, et n'en croyait rien' (chap. 30).

The scope of the satire in *Candide* is thus very large, ranging as it does over widely diverse aspects of the human scene. It is given unity, however, not merely by the fact that the various satirical themes are all related to the process of disillusionment which Candide undergoes and which forms the core of the narrative, but also by the coherent attitude which inspires it. Underlying everything in the book is Voltaire's profound horror of suffering and injustice, and his compassion for their victims. What provokes him to satire is the human conduct responsible for them, especially when the cause of it is not merely indifference to others, or cynical egoism, but ignorance, stupidity, vanity, hypocrisy, blind subservience to fashion, established custom or superstitious belief. The brutal sailor in chapter 5, who drowns the good Jacques and exploits the Lisbon earthquake as an opportunity for plunder, drunkenness and lust, is an appalling example to Candide of what human nature

C

is capable of, but he affords no occasion for satire because his conduct is at least consistent and, as he clearly tells Pangloss, he rejects all moral and rational standards. As such, he is beyond the reach of criticism. But the Dutch pastor who preaches on charity and then refuses it from sectarian intolerance (chap. 3); the University which thinks that a few burnings at the stake will stop an earthquake; the religious order vowed to poverty, humility and charity which is rich, arrogant and warlike; the petty aristocrat whose snobbery blinds him to reality and the demands of gratitude; the accepted laws and international customs which are permitted to legitimize the cruelties of war or the execution of a brave admiral for cowardice 'pour encourager les autres'; above all, the vain folly of metaphysicians who in their eagerness to propound impressive philosophical systems explaining everything in the universe fail to notice that their explanations are incompatible with simple everyday experience (or, if they do notice it, are too vain to admit it)—such subjects are material for satire because they are vulnerable to criticism on rational grounds, because they involve inconsistencies which can be shown to be absurd as well as harmful.

Behind the satire, then, there lies a rational critique. In ridiculing and attacking these human follies and cruelties Voltaire is by implication demanding more intelligent standards of conduct, greater rationality and a keener sense of reality, as well as more charity, from his fellow men. At the same time, he is asserting his faith that the human lot can be improved by the acceptance of such standards, that enlightenment is the way to happiness. This faith is given an utopian expression in the description of Eldorado, the perfect country where men live according to the rational principles of deism, where there are no priests, no monks, no law courts, and all is prosperity and happiness. Such a world is beyond the bounds of practical possibility, as Voltaire acknowledges by giving it the mythical name of Eldorado, but some progress towards it is possible. Candide achieves enlightenment through his experiences, and the little community assembled at Constantinople, if more modest in its scope and expectations than Eldorado, is inspired by the same principles.

'Cultiver notre jardin' is an essentially honest, rational and charitable activity.

Many of the characteristic features of Voltaire's style in *Candide* will by now have become apparent, for they reflect aspects of the book which we have already discussed. The whole conception of the tale as a compact adventure story in which, after the manner of the picaresque novel but in much smaller compass, the central figures are hurried along through a rapid series of encounters, necessarily commits the author to a pungent brevity of manner. The many minor characters must be hit off in a phrase, situations must be presented in a sentence or two, journeys accomplished, intervals of time passed over, without the reader's losing that sense of furious pace which is essential, yet without his feeling that the sketch is too hasty to have life. Such demands were not uncongenial to Voltaire, whose natural manner was the epigrammatic rather than the rhetorical, and whose creative powers were not richly imaginative. And his success in meeting them is considerable. A typical passage is that in which he describes the adventures of Candide and Cacambo when, after leaving the Oreillons, they try to make for Cayenne:

> Il n'était pas facile d'aller à la Cayenne; ils savaient bien à-peu-près de quel côté il fallait marcher; mais des montagnes, des fleuves, des précipices, des brigands, des sauvages, étaient partout de terribles obstacles. Leurs chevaux moururent de fatigue; leurs provisions furent consumées: ils se nourrirent un mois entier de fruits sauvages, et se trouvèrent enfin auprès d'une petite rivière bordée de cocotiers, qui soutinrent leur vie et leurs espérances [chap. 17].

Weeks of hardship and manifold dangers are here brought to life for the reader in a paragraph, by a continual emphasis upon detail which is all the more evocative for being conveyed in a word—'des précipices, des brigands, des sauvages'—and by a discreet, but repeated insistence upon the travellers' reactions—'il n'était pas facile . . .', 'de terribles obstacles', 'soutinrent leur vie et leurs espérances'. And all this is a necessary preparation for the climax of the hazardous river voyage to Eldorado and the contrasting scenes of comfort and safety which follow it.

Again, the element of parody which, we have seen, is of the essence of the tale, finds reflection in the style. It occasions, for one thing, such caricatures of the conventional rhetorical outbursts of lovers as the one already quoted: 'à quoi me servira de prolonger mes misérables jours, puisque je dois les traîner loin d'elle dans les remords et dans le désespoir?' (chap. 16). But it also permits a degree of caricature which reaches the level of fantasy. The disease-ridden Pangloss whom Candide finds in Holland makes his appearance at first anonymously, as 'un gueux', and he is a figure of, deliberately, nightmarish repulsiveness—'tout couvert de pustules, les yeux morts, le bout du nez rongé, la bouche de travers, les dents noires, et parlant de la gorge, tourmenté d'une toux violente, et crachant une dent à chaque effort' (chap. 3). Voltaire, indeed, insists upon the unreality of this vision by calling him 'le fantôme' in the next paragraph, immediately before shocking Candide, and the reader, with the revelation of the beggar's identity. This is fantasy of description which is parallel to the narrative fantasy of the resurrection of Pangloss and the Baron at the end of the tale.

The aspect of style in *Candide* which is most characteristic, however, and worth more attention than critics have commonly given it, is Voltaire's use of irony. Here, too, the manner of writing is organically related to the matter, for the central theme of *Candide*, the doctrine of optimism and its critique through the disillusionment of Candide, is one which, so to speak, spontaneously generates the ironical. Optimism, or at least the optimism of Pangloss, is essentially here a dogma, an article of faith which insists upon interpreting in a good sense, as ultimately beneficial, every event in human experience, however negative, degrading, or painful. Its natural tendency in expression is consequently towards euphemism. But neither author nor reader, nor ultimately Candide himself, shares this optimistic faith. Hence what is presented to us in the voice of optimism inevitably acquires the tone of irony: we interpret it as meaning the opposite of what it says, and the events of the story confirm for us, and convince Candide, that this is the correct interpretation. In this way, Voltaire effectively satirizes the optimists by transforming their affirmations of dogmatic faith into ironic comments on a grim reality. The reader finds himself continually echoing the words of Candide himself in a moment of disillusionment: 'Si c'est ici le meilleur des mondes possibles, que sont donc les autres?'

It is not only optimistic dogma, however, which creates such effects in *Candide*. Other satirical themes are also presented as generating irony. The barbaric primitiveness of life in Westphalia is revealed to the reader, not by any direct judgment, but through the confident pride of the inhabitants, who in their ignorance believe they live in 'le paradis terrestre'. And in the brilliant opening chapter of the book this is combined with our introduction to Pangloss and his optimism; Voltaire ironically adopts the tone of both, so that naïvety and dogmatism together give us a picture full of superlatives and at the same time wholly deflatory in its effect. 'Monsieur le baron était un des plus puissants seigneurs de la Westphalie, car son château avait une porte et des fenêtres.' Pangloss 'prouvait admirablement qu'il n'y a pas d'effet sans cause, et que dans ce meilleur des mondes possibles, le château de monseigneur le baron était le plus beau des châteaux, et madame la meilleure des baronnes possibles'. And by the same means the mock tragedy of Candide's expulsion from Thunder-ten-tronckh is enhanced: 'tout fut consterné dans le plus beau et le plus agréable des châteaux possibles'.

War, too, is a satirical theme which can be presented ironically. Here also a gap exists between euphemism and reality, between the picture of war which rulers find it useful to sponsor—gay uniforms, cheerful music, and the splendour of heroism—and the grim and cruel facts. The recruiting officers who enlist Candide into the Bulgarian army themselves use the flattering convention of military heroism ironically, as a bait, when they talk of fortune and glory; but the irony is at first lost upon the still innocent Candide—it is only a little later that, shocked by his first taste of the harsh life of the recruit, he begins to suspect the fraud: 'Candide tout stupéfait ne démêlait pas encore trop bien comment il était un héros' (chap. 2). It is in the battle-scene which opens the following chapter, however, that Voltaire most fully exploits the ironical possibilities of the subject. His description begins in conventional tones of martial splendour, which are carefully thrown into discord by the last word of the second sentence: 'Rien n'était si beau, si leste, si brillant, si bien ordonné que les deux armées. Les trompettes, les fifres, les haut-bois, les tambours, les canons formaient une harmonie telle qu'il n'y en eut jamais en enfer.' Then, the jargon of optimism is employed to lend ironical support to the conventionally euphemistic phrasing of the casualty report:

> Les canons renversèrent d'abord à-peu-près six mille hommes de chaque côté; ensuite la mousquetterie ôta du meilleur des mondes environ neuf à dix mille coquins qui en infectaient la surface. La baïonnette fut aussi la raison suffisante de la mort de quelques milliers d'hommes. Le tout pouvait bien se monter à une trentaine de mille âmes.

It is only after this, when Candide is fleeing from 'cette boucherie heroïque' while the *Te Deum* is being sung in both camps, that the realities of the situation, the dead and dying in the villages sacked 'selon les lois du droit public', are described in savage detail; and the full force of the irony is brought home to the reader.

Similar opportunities for irony are also offered by the Portuguese Inquisition, in the contrast between the supposedly beneficent purposes of the Holy Office, the redemption of heretics and the protection of divine truth, and the cruelty of its actual practices. The agents of the Inquisition treat Pangloss with extreme courtesy as they extract evidence of his heretical views:

> 'Apparemment que monsieur ne croit pas au péché originel; car si tout est au mieux, il n'y a donc eu ni chute ni punition.'—'Je demande très humblement pardon à votre excellence,' répondit Pangloss encore plus poliment, 'car la chute de l'homme et la malédiction entraient nécessairement dans le meilleur des mondes possibles.'—'Monsieur ne croit donc pas à la liberté?' dit le familier.—'Votre excellence m'excusera,' dit Pangloss . . . [chap. 5].

And this courtly tone is retained by Voltaire when he comes to describe the dungeons in which Pangloss and Candide are imprisoned: 'tous deux furent menés séparément dans des appartements d'une extrême fraîcheur, dans lesquels on n'était jamais incommodé du soleil' (chap. 6). Similarly, the aesthetic qualities and entertainment value of the auto-da-fé are ironically emphasized: the victims 'entendirent un sermon très pathé-tique, suivi d'une belle musique en faux-bourdon. Candide fut fessé en cadence pendant qu'on chantait' (chap. 6). Cunégonde was invited as a spectator: 'Je fus très bien placée; on servit aux dames des rafraîchisse-ments entre la messe et l'exécution' (chap. 8). And by the end of the ceremony Candide is in a position to compare, from experience, the value of the different benefits it has conferred upon him: 'Il s'en re-tournait se soutenant à peine, prêché, fessé, absous et béni.'

Irony, then, is here much more than one among many possible satirical devices. It forms an essential part of the whole conception of *Candide*, because the book is above all an attack on systems of thought and attitudes of mind which divorce men from reality and reason, which substitute words for facts and prefer habit to reflection. Such systems and attitudes conceal truth behind a mask; they can be most effectively dis-credited by setting the truth beside the mask and allowing the spectator to judge for himself. The rosy dogma of the optimists, the euphemistic clichés of Church and State, are thus emptied of their positive content and transformed into ironic statements, and the reader is encouraged by this spectacle to reject all such pronouncements whenever they are not sup-ported by his own experience and his own reasoning. 'Il faut cultiver notre jardin' is a motto for self-reliance in thought as well as action.

Candide thus emerges as a work of art of considerable complexity. Parody, satire, intellectual debate, all contribute their share of the material; each has its own complexity, and each amuses and interests in its own way. The range is vast, within such a small compass: not merely in subject-matter, but also in tone—from bawdy jokes at the expense of La Vieille to compassionate horror at human suffering in war and earth-quake, from ironic bitterness to the almost rhapsodical utopianism of

Eldorado. Yet for the most part these diverse elements are organically related to each other: the literary framework of parody encourages in the reader a critical alertness which is also essential for his appreciation of the central intellectual theme; the central theme itself, the disillusionment of Candide, is such that the secondary satirical themes can all take their place as agents in the process; while the distinguishing features of the style, the pungent rapidity of manner, the contrasts of scene and incident, the pervading irony, all arise naturally and inevitably from the nature of the material itself. Such organic unity is not solely the result of literary craftsmanship, however, important as that is: it has its roots much deeper in Voltaire's personality. Not merely is *Candide* a vehicle, among many others, for Voltaire's compassion for human suffering and anger at human cruelty, intolerance and stupidity; it is above all an expression of perhaps the profoundest force in his nature, the need for activity, for coming to grips with reality and leaving his own mark upon it. It was precisely this need which the static philosophy of 'optimism', unwilling to face facts and destructive of all hope, seemed most to deny; and it is understandable that in reacting against it Voltaire should marshal all the creative and critical powers at his command, and produce a masterpiece.

Background

Having proved itself still capable of attracting readers and giving them pleasure two hundred years after its first appearance, *Candide* may be felt to have achieved literary immortality. The appeal of such enduring works of art must obviously in a sense be timeless, but that does not mean that they are not better understood, and so more enjoyed, by those who are able to replace them in the historical context from which they sprang, to comprehend something of their meaning for the author and his contemporaries, to see how they are related to the preoccupations and the attitudes of their age. And this is especially true of a work of satire, intended by its author to be a weapon in a contemporary clash of ideas, ultimately to influence the course of events by its impact on men's minds. It remains for us, then, to look at *Candide* externally from this historical standpoint, and to say something, in particular, of the history of eighteenth-century 'optimism', and of the development of Voltaire's own attitude on the subject.

The problem of divine justice or theodicy, of reconciling the existence of evil and suffering with the goodness and omnipotence of God, is one that clearly is of permanent concern not only to Christian theology but also to all believers in a creator rationally conceived as a Supreme Being. And it was a problem which became particularly acute in Western Europe about the beginning of the eighteenth century. The renewed confidence in the powers of human reason which characterizes so much of European thought in the seventeenth century, from Descartes onwards, contributed to this in two main ways. In the first place, as it led philosophers like Descartes himself, Spinoza and Leibniz to conceive vast metaphysical systems in which every known feature of the universe was (ideally, at any rate) rationally accounted for and fitted into a comprehensive and coherent intellectual scheme, so also religious thinkers were impelled to emphasize the rationality of Christianity, to attempt to win or regain the allegiance of the now growing number of sceptics and freethinkers by demonstrating that Christian beliefs were entirely compatible with reason. In such an attempt, the problem of evil clearly constituted a major issue.

Secondly, the new rationalism was beginning to bear fruit where man's understanding of the world was concerned. New instruments like the telescope and the microscope, new mathematical techniques, a new awareness of the importance of experiment and observation, were making possible for the first time some scientific understanding of natural phenomena. Where formerly it had been assumed that, since the Fall, the world was predominantly given over to chaos and corruption, regularity and even purpose now began to be descried in the workings of nature. It seemed plausible to compare the universe to a watch, the most complex and delicately constructed machine of the age—a machine in which every part functioned regularly and purposefully, in accordance with the intentions of the watchmaker. If the arrangements of the Divine Watchmaker, however, proved accessible to human reason in such matters as the law of gravitation or the principles of optics (to quote the discoveries of Newton alone), the presumption seemed to follow that rational purpose pervaded every feature of the universe; and here too the problem arose as to how the existence of such manifest blemishes as evil and suffering could be reconciled with the necessary perfection of the divine scheme.

It is these two approaches to the problem, different in origin and emphasis but similar in their rationalism, which underlay respectively the two most influential and widely discussed formulations of the 'optimistic' solution, those of Leibniz and of Alexander Pope.

Leibniz's purpose in his *Essais de Théodicée* (1710: written in French) was essentially to defend the rationality of God and His creation against an attack which, in his eyes, was a potential danger to religion and to man's confidence in the divine purposes. The French Huguenot scholar and philosopher Pierre Bayle (1647–1706), a critical rather than a constructive thinker, had frequently emphasized the limitations of the human reason by drawing attention to philosophical paradoxes which appeared to admit of no rational solution; and one of these, in his view, was the problem of evil. In the articles 'Manichéens' and 'Pauliciens' of his *Dictionnaire Historique et Critique* (1697) he argued that the explanation propounded by the ancient Manichean heresy, namely that the world was the plaything of opposing gods, one good, one evil, was in fact the solution of the problem most in keeping with the facts, however illogical and incompatible with our notions of God it might be:

> Qui n'admirera et qui ne déplorera la destinée de notre raison: voilà les Manichéens qui avec une hypothèse tout-à-fait absurde et contradictoire expliquent les expériences cent fois mieux que ne font les orthodoxes, avec la supposition si juste, si nécessaire, si uniquement véritable d'un premier principe infiniment bon et tout-puissant ['Pauliciens', note E].

Leibniz's book is a systematic discussion of Bayle's views, and in it he propounds an answer to the problem of evil which is in harmony with his own wider metaphysical thinking and also supports the claims of rational theology. He sees God as subject, like man, to the laws of reason: even God cannot make two and two add up to anything but four, nor create a spherical cube. Hence, when God is considered as deciding upon the creation of the world, Leibniz envisages him as having a choice only between *possible* worlds, that is, forms of creation which do not violate the laws of reason, which do not involve logical contradiction. And among such possible worlds God in His infinite goodness has inevitably chosen the best. This 'best of all possible worlds', however, necessarily contains imperfections, and hence evil. While many evils are justifiable and even valuable as a means to good (e.g. the protective and warning function of much physical pain), other evils are merely the inevitable result of the imperfections inseparable from the status of created beings; man has limited power, limited knowledge: 'Il y a une imperfection originale dans la créature avant le péché, parce que la créature est limitée essentiellement: d'où vient qu'elle ne saurait tout savoir, et qu'elle se peut tromper et faire d'autres fautes' (*Théodicée*, I, §20). Evil of this sort is thus presented by Leibniz not as a positive force, but rather as something negative and privative; not anything willed by God, but an imperfection arising inevitably from the nature of things, and to which man must consequently reconcile himself. The fact of evil is not denied, but its presence in God's creation is morally justified and rationally accounted for.

The second version of the philosophy of optimism is linked with the name of Alexander Pope, not because he himself was an original thinker (he chiefly echoes the views of his contemporary, Bolingbroke, and the earlier English philosopher, Shaftesbury), but because he succeeded, in his *Essay on Man* (1733), in crystallizing and giving memorable expression to ideas on the subject which reflected the outlook of many contemporaries. It had become a common practice for Christian apologists to invoke the new scientific discoveries as evidence: that the marvels of the universe bear witness to God's existence and His providence is the theme of such works as the Rev. W. Derham's *Physico-Theology* (1713) and *Astro-Theology* (1715), both of which were frequently reprinted and translated into French, and of the Abbé Pluche's equally successful *Spectacle de la nature* (1732). The discovery of order and purpose in the world of nature led less orthodox thinkers, however, to conclusions incompatible with the Christian doctrine of original sin. If scientific investigation revealed the working of universal laws, the existence of rational purpose, in every phenomenon so far scrutinized, it seemed likely that greater knowledge would display the ultimate regularity and purposiveness of *everything* in the universe: that whatever now appeared as random, imperfect, evil, would be revealed as playing its necessary part in the universal order. Man's capacity for comprehending this order, it was argued, is inevitably limited by his own quite restricted part in it, but the universe as a whole is perfect, the unblemished product of the divine wisdom and omnipotence, and it is merely human ignorance

which makes us see imperfection and evil in it. Such are the views Pope
advances in the First Epistle of his *Essay on Man*:

> Cease then, nor order imperfection name:
> Our proper bliss depends on what we blame.
> Know thy own point: this kind, this due degree
> Of blindness, weakness, Heav'n bestows on thee.
> Submit.—In this or any other sphere,
> Secure to be as blest as thou canst bear:
> Safe in the hand of one disposing power,
> Or in the natal, or the mortal hour.
> All nature is but art, unknown to thee;
> All chance, direction, which thou canst not see;
> All discord, harmony not understood;
> All partial evil, universal good;
> And, spite of pride, in erring reason's spite,
> One truth is clear, Whatever is, is right.

The distinction between this view and that of Leibniz is thus a wide
one. Leibniz, starting from a theological standpoint, admits the reality
of evil but sees it as an inevitable ingredient even in the best of all possible
worlds. Pope on the other hand, adopting an approach which was of
scientific inspiration, proclaims that evil is a mere illusion, a consequence
of human ignorance. And the moral which the two writers drew from
their conclusions similarly differed, for while Leibniz wished by his
vindication of the ways of God to men to counteract the despair and
helplessness which Manicheism might provoke, and to encourage men
to collaborate actively with God in the working out of His purposes,
Pope seems to preach only passive submission to a Providence which, if
universally rational and ultimately beneficent, is also beyond man's
limited comprehension.

Such distinctions are important if we are to understand the history of
optimism, but in practice they were seldom made by the eighteenth-
century public. Pope's poem was enormously successful in France: no
less than four different translations, two of which were frequently
reprinted, appeared between 1736 and 1750; and it was very commonly,

though erroneously, supposed that Pope had been influenced by Leibniz. Interest in Leibniz, indeed, which had somewhat languished in France since his death in 1716, was revived precisely by the controversy which sprang up over Pope's poem. It is significant that the fullest discussion ever accorded to Leibniz's *Théodicée* in a French periodical appeared, not in a review of the first edition of 1710, but in 1737, the year after the publication of the first French translation of the *Essay on Man*, when the Jesuit *Mémoires de Trévoux* devoted four articles to reviewing an edition of the *Théodicée* published in 1734.

The issue at stake in the controversy was a crucial one. The optimism expressed in Pope's poem, and which was commonly supposed to be that of Leibniz also, appeared in the 1730s as a characteristically deistic view. It presented God as a rational Supreme Being, the creator of a rational, ordered, perfect universe; it clearly left no room for such notions as the Fall, original sin, Christ's atonement, redemption by divine grace, or even, in the eyes of many, for freedom of the will. And at that date deism was the commonest form assumed by the growing European movement of free thought, the strongest enemy with which the Church had to contend. The forces of orthodoxy consequently reacted vigorously, condemning such doctrines as unchristian and above all fatalistic; but their attraction remained strong in an age which tended to complacency, was impressed by the achievements of the new science, and found the rationalistic notions of deism more congenial than the dogmas of revealed religion.

If Leibniz, who was little read, became better known, and by some better thought of, as a result of this renewed French interest in optimism, his reputation scarcely benefited in France from a further development, which served nevertheless to keep his name before the public in the following two decades. Owing chiefly to Leibniz's unwillingness to publish systematic expositions of his views, his philosophy, for all its originality and importance, exercised extremely little direct influence: but early in the eighteenth century there appeared in Germany an academic disciple of Leibniz whose impact was considerable. Christian

Wolff (1679–1754), a professor in the universities of Halle and Marburg, was above all a systematizer and an expositor, developing some of Leibniz's principal conceptions into an all-embracing philosophical structure which covered every aspect of human thought, from logic to theology, from metaphysics to ethics. This he presented in lectures to students over a period of thirty years and published in some forty quarto volumes, in which his thought is set out in a rigidly organized pattern resembling that of a textbook of geometry. The apparently solid, 'mathematically' proven certainties of this arid and pedantic philosophical system had great appeal for his contemporaries, however, and before his death Wolff's philosophy had become the established orthodoxy in the universities of northern Germany.

It was in these Protestant areas of the country that many thousands of Huguenots had settled when in 1685 the revocation of the Edict of Nantes had forced them to leave France. These refugees, and especially the second generation, born in exile, while they preserved their religious traditions and their national language, also came inevitably under the influence of contemporary German movements. Some became enthusiastic Wolffians, and consequently tried to win further adherents by spreading knowledge of Wolff's system in the French-speaking world. French translations and expositions of Wolff were published in the late 1730s and the 1740s by Jean Deschamps, a little-known pastor in Berlin who later lived in London, and by the much more influential J. H. S. Formey, a Huguenot minister and professor who became the permanent Secretary of the Berlin Academy of Sciences in 1748, contributed articles to Diderot's *Encyclopédie*, and was extremely active throughout his career as a publicist and journalist. Formey's most ambitious attempt at presenting Wolff to French readers was *La Belle Wolfienne* (6 vols., 1741–53), a work which, in the early volumes at any rate, tried to emulate the conversational method of popular scientific exposition used so successfully by Fontenelle in his *Entretiens sur la pluralité des mondes habités* half a century before. But certainly more influential than this was his journalistic work. From 1734 until its disappearance in 1760 Formey was on the editorial staff of a periodical primarily concerned with presenting German literary and intellectual life to French readers, the *Bibliothèque Germanique*, and in the 1740s and '50s he was able to use it as an organ of Wolffian propaganda, consistently publishing articles and reviews in which Wolff's philosophy was expounded and put forward in a favourable light.

The positive effect of this campaign in France itself was not very great. The only French convert to Wolffianism of any significance was Voltaire's mistress, Madame Du Châtelet. Won over, at least temporarily, by the enthusiasm of a disciple of Wolff whom she employed for a time as a mathematics tutor, Samuel König, she prefaced a popular introduction to physics which she published in 1741, the *Institutions de physique*, with an outline of the metaphysical conceptions of Leibniz (including the doctrines of the *Théodicée*), 'puisées dans les ouvrages du célèbre Wolff'. The general effect, however, of such pro-Wolffian activities was at least to keep the names of Leibniz and Wolff before the French public by provoking opposition. Apart from Madame Du Châtelet's book, during the twenty years preceding *Candide* virtually nothing was published on the subject in France itself which was not hostile to the Wolffian philosophy. It appeared to most French minds as an extreme example of a kind of dogmatic speculation which the new scientific progress, based upon observed fact only, had shown to be valueless. Condillac dealt this sort of philosophy a crushing blow with his devastatingly critical *Traité des systèmes* in 1749, and D'Alembert in 1751 recorded the decease of systematic metaphysics in his *Discours préliminaire de l'Encyclopédie*: 'Le goût des systèmes, plus propre à flatter l'imagination qu'à éclairer la raison, est aujourd'hui presqu'absolument banni des bons ouvrages.'

The interest in the doctrines of optimism which Pope's *Essay on Man* had stimulated in France was thus reinforced to some extent by the attempts of Madame Du Châtelet and the Huguenot enthusiasts in Germany to attract French support for the philosophy of Leibniz and Wolff. Pope and Leibniz were continually linked together by controversialists, 'le meilleur des mondes possibles' and Pope's 'tout est bien'

('Whatever is, is right') became the catch-phrases of the discussion: but even those in France who sympathized with the optimistic solution of the problem of evil were rarely disposed to accept also the complete meta-physical system in which Wolff had embedded it. The outlines of that system became better known in France than Leibniz's own thought had ever been, thanks to the efforts of the Wolffian propagandists: but Frenchmen, it seems, if they were able now to recognize such technical phrases as 'l'harmonie préétablie', 'la raison suffisante', or 'les monades' as characteristically Leibnizian, saw no reason to take Leibnizian meta-physics seriously, and now also associated it with the pedantic aridity and prolixity of Wolff—who in these respects well exemplified the current French conception of German pedagogues and scholars.

Optimism itself, moreover, though defended by enthusiasts in Germany, continued to come under fire in France. As we have seen, the forces of religious orthodoxy condemned it, emphasizing especially the fatalistic implications which were inseparable from it; and to many men of sense it seemed less and less in accordance with the observable facts of existence—an impression which was of course enormously strengthened by the Lisbon earthquake of 1755.

We are now in a better position to understand the immediate success of *Candide*. In it Voltaire is making fun of a philosophy much discussed in France, but generally rejected there: one which aroused great interest, because it was concerned with a problem of acute importance for the age, but which had also acquired an aura of ridicule through becoming associated in the public mind with the academic jargon of German pedants and their infatuated disciples. In creating Pangloss, the German pedagogue, with his Leibnizian clichés, his irrepressible passion for metaphysical dogmatizing, and his blind devotion to optimism, Voltaire was setting up a butt for satire at which all France could laugh.

To describe the development of Voltaire's attitude to the question of optimism it is not necessary, or possible, to go back to the earliest years of his career: the successful young court poet and dramatist of the

D

Regency had as yet no serious personal concern with such profound matters as the problem of evil. Yet, with his early interest in Bayle and impatience with religious orthodoxy, he can scarcely have failed, even as a very young man, to be aware of the importance of the question. He of course read his friend Pope's *Essay on Man* as soon as it appeared in 1733, and it is noteworthy that, although he qualified his first praise of it with the remark that 'Now and then there is some obscurity' (letter, in English, to Thieriot, 24 July 1733, Best. D635), his own earliest recorded opinions on the subject, which belong to this period, are on the whole in harmony with Pope's views. In his *Lettres philosophiques* (1734) he includes an attack on Pascal which opposes to Pascal's deep sense of original sin the assertion that all is well with creation, that man, even if he has his imperfections, is nevertheless in his rightful place in the divinely created order. Pope's optimism thus had its part to play as a weapon against Christian orthodoxy where doctrines of sin and redemption were concerned; but when, a year or two later, he attempts for the first time, in his *Traité de métaphysique*, to argue seriously the case for deism, he tries to exonerate God from responsibility for evil, from charges of cruelty and injustice towards man, by a new approach. He does not follow Pope to the optimistic extreme of maintaining that all evil is a means to good, but rather asserts that man is in no position to make judgments at all on the subject. To reproach God with injustice is to apply to Him a notion which is meaningful only with reference to one man's treatment of another; to condemn creation as imperfect is absurd unless we have some more perfect universe with which to compare it; God's ways, in short, are not our ways.

Such arguments give the impression of having been sought out as a way of answering the orthodox opponents of deism, rather than as springing from any very profound conviction. And Voltaire in the 1730s had little personal inclination to take the problem very seriously. As he makes clear in his epicurean poem of 1736, *Le Mondain*, he thought the world a pleasant place: 'le paradis terrestre est où je suis'; and, without denying the existence of evil in the world (he seems to have felt, indeed, that Pope tended too easily to gloss it over), he sees little point at this stage in his career in arguing over such problems, when life offers so much to enjoy:

> Sans rechercher en vain ce que peut notre maître,
> Ce que fut notre monde, et ce qu'il devrait être,
> Observons ce qu'il est, et recueillons le fruit
> Des trésors qu'il renferme et des biens qu'il produit.
> (*Sixième Discours sur l'homme*, 1738)

Voltaire's acquaintance with the philosophy of Leibniz began effectively only in 1736, when the future Frederick the Great, at that time a devotee, sent him some French translations of Wolff's works. Further contacts undoubtedly came through the Leibnizian enthusiasm of Madame Du Châtelet, which began in 1739: it seems to have been about this date that Voltaire first acquired some knowledge of the *Théodicée*. It is clear that Voltaire rapidly lost patience with the Wolffian enthusiasts, whose pedantic metaphysical dogmatism and supreme confidence in their own speculations he found exasperating—the complete antithesis of everything he admired in Locke and Newton, with their cautious scepticism and persistent refusal to go beyond the established facts. It is Leibnizian metaphysics, not the Leibnizian doctrine of optimism, that Voltaire makes fun of at this time, however; believing no doubt, with many of his contemporaries, that Leibniz and Pope were at one on the latter subject, he would have felt no desire to attack a view with which he was then largely in sympathy.

By 1744, however, the first signs of a different attitude begin to emerge. In that year, in a bitterly mocking reply to an attack which a Wolffian professor of philosophy, L. M. Kahle of Göttingen, had made on his *Métaphysique de Newton*, Voltaire includes Leibnizian optimism in his ridicule, closing his letter with the sarcastic gibe: 'Quand vous aurez aussi démontré en vers ou autrement pourquoi tant d'hommes s'égorgent dans le meilleur des mondes possibles, je vous serai très obligé' (Best. D2945). This sense that the realities of human suffering and evil are fundamentally irreconcilable with the doctrine of optimism, that, far from making them comprehensible and tolerable, optimism merely mocks at them, is one that comes more and more to dominate Voltaire's thinking on the subject in the ensuing years, and it is this which inspires *Candide*.

In the middle and late 1740s, too, Voltaire returned to the life of a courtier at Versailles. With its continual insecurity, its petty jealousies, its frivolous demands upon his time and literary energies, the flattery and insincerity which it necessitated, such an existence soon destroyed the sense of personal contentment which had underlain his earlier epicurean sympathy with Pope. At the same time, however, he had not altogether abandoned the intellectual conviction (implicit in his sincere deism) that, the universe being rational, a rational explanation of the fact of evil must exist. The conflict between the two attitudes, the one intellectual, the other at bottom emotional and personal, emerges clearly in the first of Voltaire's *contes* to be published, *Zadig*, the earliest version of which appeared in 1747.

In this tale the central theme is the problem of destiny: not whether it exists—Voltaire by this date was a convinced determinist, and his oriental hero has the traditional fatalism of his race—but why it treats men as capriciously and unjustly as it does.

Zadig is a young man of talent and virtue, yet his career is continually beset with undeserved misfortune: both men and events seem to conspire maliciously against him. Finally, after many adventures, he is on the point of winning the hand of his beloved, Queen Astarte, only to be cheated by the treachery of his last rival, a knight in green armour whom he had defeated in single combat. Zadig can endure no more: 'Il lui échappa enfin de murmurer contre la Providence, et il fut tenté de croire que tout était gouverné par une Destinée cruelle qui opprimait les bons, et qui faisait prospérer les chevaliers verts' (chap. 17). At this climax in the story, Zadig meets a mysterious hermit, who offers to enlighten and console him. On their way together, however, the hermit baffles and horrifies Zadig by his strange behaviour: he steals from one man who offers them generous hospitality, burns down the house of another, richly rewards those who treat them badly, and finally recompenses a hospitable and virtuous widow by deliberately drowning her nephew. The hermit, who has access to the book of destiny, is able to show Zadig how each of these actions was in fact beneficial, in spite of appearances: even the murder of the nephew was for the best, for if the boy had lived he would have killed his aunt, and Zadig too! The hermit now reveals himself to be the angel Jesrad, and the seal of supernatural authority seems to be set upon the interpretation of the workings of destiny which these episodes imply: whatever man, with his limited knowledge, may think, all is in fact for the best when it is seen from the transcendental viewpoint available to celestial beings.

Zadig, however, is not satisfied with these explanations. He continues to ask questions: would it not have been better to have changed the boy's destiny, and made him virtuous, rather than to have drowned him? Why should crime and unhappiness be necessary at all? What if there were only goodness, and no evil? These questions the angel tries to answer by again insisting upon the ultimate justice and beneficence of Providence: 'Les méchants, répondit Jesrad, sont toujours malheureux. Ils servent à éprouver un petit nombre de justes répandus sur la terre, et il n'y a point de mal dont il ne naisse un bien' (chap. 18). And to the question why evil exists at all, he answers merely that without evil this world would be a different world, nearer to the divine perfection, occupying a different place in the universal order from that to which God has in fact assigned it. Man must merely submit, and accept the purposes of Providence, which he cannot hope to understand. Zadig, inevitably, finds these answers unsatisfactory; but he is given no further opportunity for argument: ' "Mais," dit Zadig . . . Comme il disait Mais, l'Ange prenait déjà son vol vers la dixième sphère.'

From a transcendental standpoint, Voltaire seems here to be implying, it may well be true that the universe is rationally and beneficently ordered, but for the individual this can never be more than a matter of faith. The sense of personal injustice and unmerited affliction remains and the reality of suffering is not mitigated by such remote and meta-physical considerations.

It is upon the inescapable fact of human suffering that Voltaire now begins to place the greatest emphasis in his treatment of the subject. In *Babouc* (1748), where he is concerned chiefly with satirizing French society and its institutions, he concludes, indeed, that 'si tout n'est pas bien, tout est passable'; but in the following year in another tale, *Memnon*, he returns to the dilemma of *Zadig*. Memnon too, after a horrifying series of undeserved misfortunes, including the loss of an eye, is con-fronted with an angelic mentor. He complains to him that this world must surely be the Bedlam of the universe—

> Pas tout-à-fait, dit l'esprit; mais il en approche: il faut que tout soit en sa place. Hé mais, dit Memnon, certains poètes, certains philosophes, ont donc grand tort de dire que *tout est bien*?—Ils ont grande raison, dit le philosophe de là-haut, en considérant l'arrangement de l'univers entier.—Ah! je ne croirai cela, répliqua le pauvre Memnon, que quand je ne serai plus borgne.

In this and the following years, moreover, Voltaire's own experiences led him to take an increasingly gloomy view of life, and strengthened his awareness of human suffering. The death of Madame Du Châtelet in 1749, the disappointment of his hopes for a congenial existence in an atmosphere of intellectual freedom at the Prussian court, the humilia-tions to which he was subjected when the inevitable break with Frederick came in 1753, his subsequent wanderings and ill-health: all this combined to create a pessimistic mood which is clearly reflected in Voltaire's correspondence, especially in the years 1752–5. All he seeks for himself is a refuge from the world's ills, a haven where he may enjoy in his now declining years some small measure of tranquillity. It is interesting to see Voltaire, in a poem written in March 1755, describing his hopes on taking possession of his new home at 'Les Délices', near Geneva (the house which to-day is occupied by the 'Institut et Musée Voltaire'); the garden of *Candide* is already beginning to take shape:

O maison d'Aristippe! O jardins d'Épicure!
. . . .
Empire de Pomone et de Flore sa sœur,
    Recevez votre possesseur;
Qu'il soit, ainsi que vous, solitaire et tranquille.
Je ne me vante point d'avoir en cet asile
    Rencontré le parfait bonheur;
Il n'est point retiré dans le fond d'un bocage;
    Il est encor moins chez les rois;
    Il n'est pas même chez le sage:
De cette courte vie il n'est point le partage;
Il faut y renoncer; mais on peut quelquefois
    Embrasser au moins son image.

In these circumstances, the Lisbon earthquake in November of that year seemed above all a confirmation of Voltaire's ideas, a further proof that 'la destinée se joue des hommes' and that the theories of the optimists were far too glib. His *Poème sur le désastre de Lisbonne* is not only a cry of horror at human suffering, but also a protest against those who, with their slogan 'Tout est bien', would shrug off such suffering as a necessary ingredient in the divinely appointed order. Voltaire now insists that, in the face of a natural disaster of such magnitude, all the stock solutions of the problem of evil are unconvincing: the existence of such misery in a world created by a just and omnipotent God is simply incomprehensible. But the worst feature of optimism, Voltaire here maintains, is that by insisting on the rational perfection of the world as it is, by saying that 'tout est bien' here and now, it is in fact denying man any hope of improvement for the future, and thereby making life intolerable. The point is given an orthodox Christian emphasis, for publication, by being linked to the idea of hope for the life to come rather than for life on earth, but the force of Voltaire's criticism is not thereby weakened:

Nos chagrins, nos regrets, nos pertes sont sans nombre.
Le passé n'est pour nous qu'un triste souvenir;
Le présent est affreux s'il n'est point d'avenir,
Si la nuit du tombeau détruit l'être qui pense.
Un jour tout sera bien, voilà notre espérance,

Tout est bien aujourd'hui, voilà l'illusion.
Les sages me trompaient, et Dieu seul a raison.

Again, we are at the source of an idea central to *Candide*. It is hope, the hope of future happiness with Cunégonde, which supports Candide in his wanderings; and it is hope, of a less ambitious if more solid sort, which still inspires the labours of the little community at Constantinople.

The *Poème sur le désastre de Lisbonne*, however, as its preface makes clear, is primarily a critique of Pope's *Essay on Man*. The Leibnizianism which holds the centre of the stage in *Candide* plays no part here, and had, indeed, received very little emphasis in any of Voltaire's earlier discussions of the subject. Events in 1756, however, were to take Voltaire's thoughts again to Germany and to remind him of the German optimists and their theories.

The outbreak of the Seven Years' War in the summer of 1756 brought Germany into the forefront of events, and the long series of campaigns there during the ensuing years, with the devastation and poverty they brought in their train, gave that country the melancholy distinction of becoming the outstanding current example of extreme human misery. Voltaire himself was acutely conscious of this suffering, for he knew the country, had friends there who were involved, and of course had been on intimate terms with the German ruler chiefly concerned, Frederick the Great. Even more than those of the Lisbon earthquake, then, the horrors of the Seven Years' War had a personal immediacy for Voltaire which would by itself perhaps suffice to explain their appearance in *Candide*. But they are also relevant to the theme of the book in another, and uniquely direct, way: Voltaire was not insensitive to the irony of a situation in which the country which was *par excellence* the home of optimism had itself become that doctrine's most striking refutation. Rossbach and Leuthen and their aftermath formed a bitter contrast with the serene optimism of the Wolffians of Göttingen and Halle. Voltaire's correspondence at this period, and especially his letters to one of his German friends who had Wolffian sympathies, the Duchess of Saxe-Gotha, is sprinkled with sardonic allusions to Leibnizianism. In October

1756, after news of a Prussian victory, he writes: 'Voilà déjà environ vingt mille hommes morts pour cette querelle, dans laquelle aucun d'eux n'avait la moindre part. C'est encore un des agréments du meilleur des mondes possibles' (Best. D7023). And later, on 4 January 1758, at a time when he may well have been on the point of beginning *Candide*, he writes her a letter in the form of a comic proclamation to the mercenary troops occupying the Duchess's territories:

> A tous croates, pandours, housards . . . : il ne doit être rien de commun entre Mme la duchesse de Gotha et vous, vilains pandours . . . vous cherchez à rendre ce monde-ci le plus abominable des mondes possibles, et elle voudrait qu'il fût le meilleur. Il le serait sans doute, si elle en était la maîtresse. Il est vrai qu'elle est un peu embarrassée avec le système de Leibniz; elle ne sait comment faire, avec tant de mal physique et moral, pour vous prouver l'optimisme; mais c'est vous qui en êtes cause, maudits housards . . . [Best. D7554].

The setting and themes of *Candide* are thus of immediate personal relevance to Voltaire's own thought and experience. The intellectual problem which it discusses is one that had serious significance for him, for it was created by the conflict between the realities of life as he had himself experienced and observed them, and the implications of that belief in a rational God to which he was sincerely committed. His hostility to the optimist solution, though he found the optimists exasperating for other reasons too, springs also from the depths of his personality. He clearly sees that optimism is a doctrine of despair: by denying the possibility of improvement in a world in which, already, 'tout est bien', it reduces man to passive acquiescence in his misfortunes; while Voltaire, even at his gloomiest, remains a man of energy, for whom life is meaningless and worthless if it is not a struggle—if it does not offer the individual some prospect of successful effort to escape from suffering and improve his condition. Finally, the historical events of the 1750s combined with his own misfortunes to give depth and immediacy to his compassion for suffering humanity, and at the same time provided him, in war-torn Germany, with a supremely ironic example of the follies of optimism.

Bibliographical Note

1. TEXTS

The standard edition of Voltaire is that edited by L. Moland— *Œuvres complètes de Voltaire*, Paris, Garnier, 1877–85, 52 vols. For the correspondence, however, this has been superseded by Th. Besterman, *Voltaire's Correspondence*, Geneva, Institut et Musée Voltaire, 1953–65, 107 vols. A new edition of *The Complete Works of Voltaire*, ed. Th. Besterman *et al.*, is now in hand, and includes a more complete edition of the *Correspondence* (Geneva, Institut et Musée Voltaire; Thorpe Mandeville, The Voltaire Foundation, 1968–).

The critical edition of *Candide* by A. Morize (Paris, Hachette, 1913: reissued, 1931, 1957) remains indispensable, but valuable additional material is to be found in the later critical edition by R. Pomeau (Paris, Nizet, 1959).

Popular reprints of *Candide* are legion. Two useful annotated editions are those by O. R. Taylor (Oxford, Blackwell, 1941) and by J. H. Brumfitt (Oxford University Press, 1968). For those who wish to read more of Voltaire's prose fiction, there is an excellent complete collection in one volume in the 'Classiques Garnier' series (Voltaire, *Romans et Contes*, ed. H. Bénac) and an annotated selection, ed. H. T. Mason, *Zadig and other stories* (Oxford University Press, 1971).

2. CRITICISM

The definitive biography of Voltaire has still to be written. The fullest factual account of his career, though the treatment is anecdotal, remains the eight-volume work by G. Desnoiresterres, *Voltaire et la société française au XVIIIe siècle* (Paris, Didier, 1869–76). The major recent biographical and critical study is Th. Besterman, *Voltaire* (London, Longman, 1969).

There are, however, several good brief introductions to Voltaire. Gustave Lanson's *Voltaire* (Paris, Hachette, 1906; revised R. Pomeau, 1960) is still in many ways unsurpassed, but R. Naves's *Voltaire, l'homme et l'œuvre* (Paris, Boivin, 1942) is also excellent, and there is a lively English book by H. N. Brailsford (*Voltaire*, London, Butterworth, 1935; Oxford University Press, 1963). R. Pomeau, *Voltaire par lui-même* (Paris, Éditions du Seuil, 1955) includes a perceptive general essay, extracts from the works, and fascinating illustrations.

Two more specialized studies of Voltaire's thought may be mentioned: P. Sakmann, *Voltaires Geistesart und Gedankenwelt* (Stuttgart, Frommann, 1910), and N. L. Torrey, *The Spirit of Voltaire* (New York, Columbia University Press, 1938; Oxford, Marston Press, 1963). R. Pomeau has also published a major work on *La Religion de Voltaire* (Paris, Nizet, 1956, 2nd edition 1969).

The development of Voltaire's attitude to optimism is discussed in: W. H. Barber, *Leibniz in France* (Oxford, Clarendon Press, 1955). There is an illuminating account of the European repercussions of the disaster of 1755 in Sir Thomas Kendrick's book *The Lisbon Earthquake* (London, Methuen, 1956).

J. van den Heuvel, *Voltaire dans ses contes* (Paris, Armand Colin, 1967) is a stimulating, if speculative, study of the tales as reflections of Voltaire's personality and experience.

Index